Ambushed
And
Abused
By A.R. Murray

This book is dedicated to all the women and girls who have had to go through this scary and demeaning situation alone.

There is always help, so please be brave enough to tell someone. You have nothing to be ashamed of and know that it wasn't your fault.

1

Amy's Story:

I remember playing hide and go seek with the neighborhood children. As the number of children dwindled after reaching base, they went home. It looked like a storm was coming and they were in a hurry to get home.

Only two people were left to finish the game and that was A.J. Thompson and I. A.J. was four years older than me. I was 10 years old at the time.

I told A.J. that I was tired, it was getting ready to rain and I wanted to go home. He told me that the game isn't over until everybody is caught and that we were going to finish the game. He told me that since I was the last one, the game should be finished quickly. As the clouds grew darker grew darker and it started to sprinkle, I told A.J. that it is raining and I didn't want to get wet. Tired of me protesting, he told me that if I came to the tree we would call the game a draw.

In my mind I thought anything to let me go home. I didn't realize at the time that I could go home anytime I felt like it. The child in me just wanted the game to be over. So, I went over to the tree and touched it the same time that A.J. did. As I was getting ready to head home, A.J. caught my hand and asked if he could have a kiss. I told him no. He said that if I kissed him, he would let the game be over.

At this point, I was getting scared

because A.J. was so much older. "The game will be over if you just give me one kiss at the tree." That's all he kept repeating as if it were a nursery rhyme or something.

I sat down at the base of the tree and his face came towards mine as I puckered up expecting to touch lips but, A.J. swiftly opened his mouth and used his tongue to force mine open. As I tried to push him away, his tight grip held me in place and I couldn't move. The next thing I knew, he was reaching under my shirt and fondling my developing breast and then in one

swift movement he had raised up my

shirt and starting kissing my them.

Then he started sucking on them and

the sensation was painful. I was

begging him to stop but he acted like

he didn't hear me or he didn't want to

hear me. As I started crying his mouth

covered mine again and then suddenly

I heard my mother calling for me. She

couldn't see what was happening to

me under the tree because it was dark

from the storm clouds and it was late

in the evening.

A.J. was startled into stopping and looking wildly at me. He told me that I better not tell anybody what had happened. He said it in a way that sounded like a threat and that lead me to believe something worse would happen if I did tell.

I just shook away from him and ran while fixing my clothes on the way home. When I was inside I felt safe. I had tears coming down my face and my mother took notice right away. She asked if I had lost in the game that I was playing since I was the last to come in. I started to cry harder and just ran into her arms. As the tears kept coming, I told her everything that happened after the game and the threat that A.J. had given. She was silent for a few minutes as if she was trying to comprehend everything her young daughter had just told her. She asked me to explain everything again and to go slowly and be very specific about the details.

After my story was over for the second time Mom went over to the phone and called A.J.'s house and asked to speak with his father. She had

relayed everything I told her to him

and while speaking to him she was

extremely upset because she was

raising her voice so loud that it could

be heard from my bedroom. She hung

up the phone and told me that I didn't

have to worry about A.J. anymore.

I never knew what happened to

him after that but he never crossed my

path again. Looking back, I was glad

that I had told my mother what

happened but my heart just breaks for

all the other girls and women who

never tell.

2

Linda's Story:

My family and I were on vacation at the beach and Greg, my husband, was still on the beach with our daughters. I had decided to go to our hotel room early to clean up before dinner. We hadn't been on vacation in a couple of years due to Greg's work schedule so when we had the chance, we took it gratefully. I wanted to be dressed and ready so I could dress the girls when they came up later.

I was in the shower and heard a knock at the door. At first I ignored it because I figured that it couldn't be Greg and the girls because he had the other room key. I had finished my shower and as I was coming into the bedroom when I heard another knock at the door. I was wrapped in a towel and went to the door. I asked who it was and I heard a faint room service as an answer. I figured they were bringing fresh towels so I barely got the door open when a strange man burst through the door. He was dressed as one of the housekeeping staff but he wasn't. I told him to get out but he shut the door behind him and just kept coming towards me. Before I could yell, he had covered my mouth with one hand and in one move he had removed my towel and tossed me on the bed.

He just stood over me staring at my body and said that he had been watching me since we arrived three days ago. He said that he had even greeted me but I hadn't noticed him.

He told me that I had a nice family and that my husband was a very lucky man.

Terror had struck inside me from the stares this man was giving me. I asked him not to hurt me and that my husband would be back at any moment. I was trying to scare him off but it didn't work. The next thing I knew he was on top of me and I was trying to fight him off. While one hand and the weight of his body was pinning me down, the other hand was feeling for his zipper and invading my body trying to place himself inside me. As he began thrusting inside me I tried to scream and that's when he reached for the towel that he had taken off me and stuffed in my mouth. I was shaking my head back and forth no but he took no notice.

He told me how beautiful I was and as he was assaulting my breasts, I kept trying to scream. In the middle of the attack, he stopped suddenly and told me not to move and went into the bathroom. In no time he came back with two bath towels and tied my hands. Once I was tied, he spread my

legs and performed oral sex on me and

the smell of him sickened me. I could

feel him tearing at the fragile skin of

my womanhood. He kept repeating

how good I tasted and how lucky my

husband was. I was praying that this

was a bad dream and at any minute I

would wake up. He returned back on

top of me and while he continued

assaulting me, my mind was

wondering back to Greg and the girls

and my not wanting them to see what

was taking place. As suddenly as he

started, my attacker stopped. He ejaculated in a towel so that he left no evidence and as he took one last look at me, he took the towel and left me on the bed.

I didn't move for a couple of minutes because I was scared that he would come back. When I felt it was safe, I untied myself and went to the door and double locked it. I slid down to the floor and cried. During my crying jag I thought of Greg and the girls…they could be up here any minute!

I cleaned up the room and took another quick shower and dressed. I did think about calling the police before I took my shower but I couldn't do it to Greg or the girls and ruin our vacation. I just went on like nothing happened.

A half hour later, Greg and the girls came in. Grace was 4 and Sasha was 6 and they both were trying to tell me what they had done while they were on the beach.

As the girls were talking to me, Greg went to take a shower and asked if I would call housekeeping so they could bring up more towels. When he said that I went numb and Greg asked if anything was wrong. I made up an excuse about being hungry and that I would call housekeeping as soon as possible.

When housekeeping dropped off the extra towels, I asked the lady working if she knew of the man that I described as my attacker. She told me that no one of that description worked at the hotel. My blood ran cold.

After a few more days I kept

looking out for the man who attacked me everywhere we went. I became more nervous than usual and when Greg noticed, I would blame it on being tired.

Finally it was time to go home. The girls were unhappy but I couldn't get packed fast enough for all of us. Before leaving the hotel, Greg went to the lobby to pick up a morning paper and on the front page was a picture and the headline that read, "Hotel Rapist Caught!" Greg showed me the paper and there was the picture my rapist.

The paper read that he would dress in

housekeeping uniforms and use the

ploy to knock on his victim's doors.

Greg stated that you're not safe

anywhere nowadays, but I just felt the

weight of the world lift from my

shoulders and enjoyed the ride home.

3

Katrina's Story:

Sheldon and I had been dating for a couple of weeks now and we were beginning to get closer. We had the same things in common. We loved to go to the movies, swim and read. I thought that we were the perfect couple.

My parents adored him. When we weren't together they would think that something was wrong and ask about him. I would tell my parents that we weren't joined at the hip and

that we liked our own space

sometimes. They would just laugh.

At school my classmates also

thought that we were the perfect

couple. Since we were seniors in high

school, some of my girlfriends thought

we had taken our relationship to the

next level. I told them that I wasn't

ready for that and my decision was

respected by Sheldon. They were

really jealous knowing that he cared

that much about me. Eight months

into the relationship, nothing much had

changed between Sheldon and me. We

wouldn't see each other on the

weekends until later in the afternoons

and then we would go out; mostly to

the movies and then we would take a

drive and find a place to be alone. On

this particular day though things were

different.

   After the usual movie, Sheldon

wanted to drive out to the country. He

stated that he was getting tired of the

same old city traffic and that you could

see the stars better in the country. I

didn't see anything wrong with a

change of scenery but I also noticed

Sheldon didn't really seem like

himself tonight. I thought the drive

would do him some good and once we

got settled he would tell me what was

wrong.

We said very little on the drive

but Sheldon was right about getting

away from the city. It was so quiet in

the country and you could see the stars

better than in the city because there

were hardly any street lights.

Once we found a place to park, it

was dark and there didn't seem to be a

house to be found anywhere.

We got in the back seat the way we usually do to see the stars from the sunroof. As we started to snuggle and kiss, Sheldon's hands began to roam in different places on my body than normal. I started to feel uncomfortable and pushed his hands away while we were still kissing but he was very persistent. I finally stopped kissing him long enough to ask him what his problem was and that I wasn't ready to take that step.   He asked me if he had been a good boyfriend and hadn't he always been there for me? I told him that he had been good to me but I thought we were going to wait until we both thought the time was right.

He told me that the time was right now…and all of a sudden he got this wild look in is eyes and pushed me down in the seat. I heard and felt my shirt being ripped and my skirt being pushed up. I was yelling for him to stop and trying to get him off me. He had his fingers ripping at my panties and he told me to shut up.

I tried to slap him but he slapped

me back and I was dazed. I felt him enter me and he started kissing me on my busted lips. He was telling me how much he loved me and how much he wanted to be with me. When it over, my favorite shirt had buttons missing, the bra I had on was opened in the front and I felt pain and wetness between my legs.

I couldn't believe the person I loved would do something like this to me. He was already dressed and ready to go home. I looked at him in disbelief but the pain between my legs told me that this was very real.

As we started back home, nothing was said between us and when he pulled into my driveway, I went running into my house. Sheldon called after me but I was scared and through with him. He even had the nerve to say that he loved me out of the window of the car.

I knew what he did was wrong and if he didn't know it, he would soon find out. Fortunately, my parents were asleep. When I saw Sheldon's car go down the street, I got my keys and headed straight for the hospital.

When I arrived at the emergency entrance, I went to the nurse's station and asked to see a doctor. The nurse there barely noticed me until I told her that I had been raped. Her eyes opened wide when she saw my swollen eye and lip. She quickly got up and went for a doctor. She told me that my parents would have to be notified since I was still a minor. The police were called and the doctor told me that a rape kit exam would have to be performed and I agreed.

By the time the exam was over, my parents were waiting to see me. My father and mother were horrified when they saw me. Dad wanted to know who had done this to me and when I said Sheldon he had a look of disbelief on his face. Then it turned red.

Physically I was sore and swollen but mentally I had to pull myself together and remember that I hadn't done anything to deserve this and Sheldon would pay for the pain he had caused. When we left the hospital, my father drove one car home and I rode with my mother in the other car.

Once I was home my mother wanted me to go straight to bed to rest. I stayed out of school for a few days until I was ready to face people again. When I did go back, the first person I saw was Sheldon. He wanted to know where I had been and why I wasn't answering his phone calls.

I looked over my shoulder and told him to ask them. Behind me were my parents, his parents and the police. He was arrested for rape. I also had a restraining order on him until he went to court. So much for his clean cut image.

Looks can be deceiving. I wasn't going to be a victim and I wasn't going to live in fear of him. I've seen it happen to too many girls and it wasn't going to happen to me. A month later, I had my parents enroll me into a basic self defense class. I enjoyed it so much that after I had finished the course, I later enrolled in a Tae Kwon Do class at the local YMCA. I recommend it to all girls who are dating. You can start class as soon as five years old. The sooner the better I always say.

Even though we are suppose to be the weaker sex, we have the right not to be abused.

What is most important in all of this is that no matter how a woman dresses or acts, it is not an open invitation for a man to take advantage of her. If you should see a woman in a situation where she is being harassed, get help immediately. You can even remain anonymous but please get help.

Wouldn't you want someone to do the same for you.

When you are on a date and you start to feel uncomfortable with the situation, let your date know. Remember no means no. If the point still doesn't get across yell, scream or cause a scene until help arrives.

This would be a good time to carry a whistle and keep your purse weighted. Mine is so heavy with regular everyday things, I could use it as a lethal weapon.

On a closing note, when walking

at night make sure that there are at least two or more people walking your way in a group. This goes for walking around schools, going shopping and just going out at night. If you are one who likes to go jogging in the early morning or late evenings, this would be a good time to find a partner to go with you or you could always invest in one of man's best friends. Most people are scared of dogs no matter how big or small they happen to be, they still bark, bite and protect their owner. Stay aware of your surroundings at all times. Anything and I mean anything that doesn't feel right to you, find the nearest telephone. If you don't own a cell phone make that an investment or find an open place of business. It will be well lit and you can ask for help or call the police. It is better to be embarrassed by a false alarm than the alternative.

Pass this information along to anybody that you consider to be in a dangerous place or situation.

Be prepared and stay prepared for anything. Don't be the victim but the victor! My prayer for you is that you will always feel safe, secure and on guard at all times.

The information in this book was very important. I wrote it for teens who were dating and those who are beginning to date.

My goal was to make this into a pamphlet but no one would publish it because I was told that there wasn't a market for this kind of information. I was also told that the contents were too explicit. This information shouldn't be kept quiet! It needs to be told and what was in this book has been heard

by teenagers before and by association

of their peer groups. In fact, they

probably know more than that.

Young people don't be fooled.

That's why I wrote this. Listen to your

parents about what they think of your

young man. Always be open and

honest with them. You can tell them

anything. It probably would be

something that they have experienced

themselves. The young man that you

maybe attracted to at school, could be

the person that intends to do to you

serious harm if you go out on a date.

I wrote this because I want you to be prepared and at least know that there are simple things that you could do to protect yourself. Enjoy your dating experience. It is the most enjoyable time of your life but that doesn't mean you can't be aware at the same time. Always be safe.